RIPPLE EFFECT

NEW AND SELECTED POEMS
BY ELAINE EQUI

COFFEE HOUSE PRESS

Minneapolis

Coffee House Press books are available to the trade through our primary distributor, Consortium Book Sales & Distribution, 1045 Westgate Drive, Saint Paul, MN 55114. For personal orders, catalogs, or other information, write to: Coffee House Press, 27 North Fourth Street, Suite 400, Minneapolis, MN 55401.

Coffee House Press is a nonprofit literary publishing house. Support from private foundations, corporate giving programs, government programs, and generous individuals helps make the publication of our books possible. We gratefully acknowledge their support in detail in the back of this book.

Library of Congress Cataloging-in-Publication Data

Equi, Elaine.
Ripple effect : new & selected poems / by Elaine Equi.
p. cm.
ISBN-13: 978-1-56689-197-4 (alk. paper)
ISBN-10: 1-56689-197-3 (alk. paper)
I. Title.

PS3555.Q5R57 2007
811'.54—dc22

2006039246
FIRST EDITION | FIRST PRINTING
1 3 5 7 9 8 6 4 2
Printed in the United States

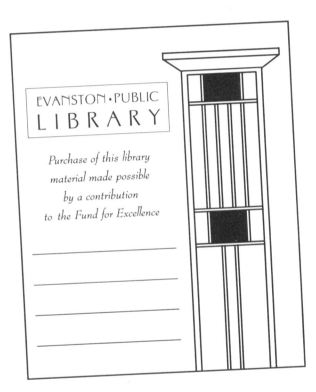

NEW WORK

FROM *SURFACE TENSION*

FROM *DECOY*

FROM *VOICE-OVER*

FROM *THE CLOUD OF KNOWABLE THINGS*

EARLY WORK

ABOUT THE ORDER

Most of these poems are from other books published by Coffee House Press. In deciding on a sequence, I've chosen to start with new work, and then, rather than simply scrolling backwards chronologically, I go instead to my very first Coffee House book, *Surface Tension*, published in 1989. That was a pivotal year for me because in addition to having a book out, I had also recently moved to New York City. The combination of a stimulating new environment with the security of having found a new press was enough to generate a lot of writing—enough in fact, to fill the next three books. The final section, Early Work, contains a selection of my B.C. (before Coffee House) poems. All but one of them were written in Chicago, which is where I'm from and not without its own charm. Over the years, I've had the pleasure of working with some of the edgiest, most adventurous, and generous editors around. A shout-out and heartfelt thanks to them here.

—E.E.

NEW WORK

TODAY IS THE FIRST DAY
OF THE REST OF YOUR LIFE

I live in the moment and cannot go elsewhere even if I wished,
however vertically I lift my gaze. I buy only enough food,
gather only enough manna to last the day. The elves make quite
a racket in the middle of the night, arguing or shrieking with
wild laughter, as they cobble together, from the footprints
of countless strangers, a final pair of shoes. Truly many
have stood where I stand, and I understand them. A long
time ago I made a solemn vow to do something not unrelated
to this. The war is peaceful—happy with its war whoops
and heavy-lidded, bellicose eyes. No one can quarrel with it.
No one can say anything to you anymore. The present
is a gift we give ourselves, its ribbon tied in a Gordian knot.
So make good use of this rampant paranoia. Spend your
cynicism where it's needed most. And while you are at it,
today's hymn can be found on p.163 of our songbooks.

HEIGH-HO, HEIGH-HO

Trudging through the long lobby
lined with mirrors enforces rehearsal.
You might say of whatever you were thinking
on the elevator—by the time you've reached
the door, you've thought about it too much.
There is a sense of subliminal self-consciousness
added to the normal amount of baggage you carry—
like having to walk through the 20th century
every day to get to work in the 21st.

Epic Mountain Hoax

Always a question of scale
fanning the flames of music.

Temple of crumbs.
Stalwart microcosms.

Swerps of brazen heroes
coup de grease.

Singularly panoptic delirium.

Tales of the mogul
lost in space.

What are you not doing down there—
the sky seems to say.

I am climbing
a flat surface (hence the difficulty)

with a sack of juicy fears—
I mean pears!

Whatever I told you yesterday wasn't me.
I was mixed up.

Today I can separate,
subtract myself better from the landscape.

MOUNTAIN TO MOUNTAIN

Marriage of mountains—

in the death valley of your shadow,
            I'll fry an egg.

Big Tit Mountain
Marlboro Country

Shangri-La-La
Mountain Dew

Iron Mountain
Sugarloaf

One day I'll climb your hunchback ladder—

a twitchy, twangy, tangy green.

I could move if I wanted,
says one mountain
                wavering to another.

But we are not like rain—
here one day, gone the next.

Be strong, stubborn mountain.

Stay fixated on yourself.

MONO-POLYTHEISM

for Dick Higgins

many gods
one country

one country
one god

many gods
many countries

one god
many countries

no god
no countries

no many
no god

many countries
one many

many many
no one

god's country
poly-mono

poly-poly
mono-poly

monopoly heaven
united states of hell

one heaven
many devils

many heavens
one devil

one devil
many hells

many gods
one devil

no god
many hells

INVOCATION

Come Inspiration,

sweet as two beautiful hookers
in a dream.

Don't go girls—

even if you don't know a thing
about poetry,

at least help me decide
what to wear.

A PERFECT SHADOW

in the gymnasium
where breath and machine

are linked.
All of us

rowing, lifting,
moving as one.

I have slipped
into its sunny rhythm

and now I am gone
too. Oh clock, you speak

but for a moment
no one hears your bird,

lion, cornice,
flag flapping its wings.

Oh clock!
Oh clock!

$1 Exceptional Coffee

for Allan Kornblum

Ace of cups.

Fountain of
a newborn cry.

Under genial
thumb-piano trees,

one sees
freakish beauties
of every stripe.

To the right,
a classical equation
resolves itself tranquilly.

To the left,
a stunning dark
girl knits darkly
and obsessively.

No one loses
(except what they want to)
in this resurrection casino.

All come away
empty-handed and free.

ULTRA-CONFESSIONAL

I'm a bit of a masochist, not much of a singer—if I had a hammer, I'd only hurt myself. My father did not think enough of me to molest me. For years, I lived with the shame of it and did not have the energy to create multiple personalities or develop an eating disorder, which has always seemed to me a pleasant way to while away the day, regulating incoming and outgoing in terms of something concrete as food or excrement.

I admit I used to like to smoke three packs a day wrapping myself in an opalescent carapace of fog and being always as in Victorian novels on the verge of swooning, particularly when climbing stairs. Then for a brief spell, during most of my teenage years, I was in love with shoplifting. It was the sex glue in my adolescent girl-on-girl world. One of those never-enough places where I allowed myself excess—hungry open pockets and purse gobbling perfume, candy, all the imagined gifts an imaginary lover should give. Going out with boys, surprisingly, proved to be an inexplicably simple solution.

But then it is so typical of me to have gone and become addicted not to heroin or gambling, but humiliatingly, to aspirin, craving their cool, white gloved hands at all hours—a headache being just another word for reality. Looking back, I'd like to say I wish I had done more evil than good, but it isn't true. Forgive me, for my sins are mediocre. My trances ordinary in every way.

1 + 1 = 3

Saltlick
tit
of the infinite

Heard
enough
of your silence

Gold
fisheyes
in aquarium glasses

Lightgeist
iceberg
blackboard and cigarette

Lamps
broken:
the show-off guiding-light

River
runs
through a bullet

Back
at
the scenic sawmill

Karmic
weenie-roast
bonfires of memorabilia

History
makes
many bad movies

Mirrors
transform
us into ourselves

CALCIUM RUSH

My bones are growing stronger.
I feel them flexing their rippling marrow
high on the leafy milk of calcium.
Tomorrow I may be able to read
thoughts unthinkable today.
I will moo through the melodious
corridors of lanky buildings
and the skyline will lengthen.
My teeth grow sharper too.

GRADUALLY, GILLS

merge
      emerging

into the antediluvian
        bloodstream.

Transposed
air is water;

water,
      air—

a busy, frizzy
bringing and brought

behind the somehow seductive
fanfare of fins.

O for a menial task
to preoccupy me
while the big picture
resolves itself

and evolution completes
its long day.

It's like being inside
a rainy aquarium

or the watershed
of a giant teardrop.

Dry water,
       liquid land.

Poems are paperweights,

ballast to keep our words
from floating away.

AMBIEN

What did I just—
did I just ask you? What
did I say? I said that yesterday?
I thought I dreamt—
it also seems like milk,
something about milk.
I must have broken it.
That's Nutella on the light switch?
I should never answer e-mails after midnight.
Those are definitely raisins on the floor.
Never, never again.
I'll just take my pill and go right to sleep.
I'll wait until I'm already asleep to swallow it.
Wait, did I just take a pill?
You were here.
Did I just go into the other room?
Did you see me do that?

THE PILL'S OVAL PORTRAIT

Chemical twin
neither happy nor sad

beneath your pink bonnet,
yellow halo,

lozenges of displaced anger,
hexagons of grief.

I have been highly productive
maintaining a certain uncertainty,

and I have translated myself entirely
into a language I do not understand.

In a temple of science, behind these amazing
red, spiked flowers (corpuscles?)

new pills are being born each day.
They will marry and take jobs away

from those who do not take them.
Years from now, we will marvel

at the crudeness,   remote,
that the economy needed to grow

so busily passive. Just one of not
too many ways of being in the world.

ETUDES

Autumn is a solitude.
Winter is a fortitude.
Spring is an altitude.
Summer is an attitude.

Summer is a multitude.
Autumn is an aptitude.
Winter is a quaalude.
Spring is a prelude.

Spring is a lassitude.
Summer is a longitude.
Autumn is a gratitude.
Winter is an interlude.

Winter is a beatitude.
Spring is a platitude.
Summer is a verisimilitude.
Autumn is a semi-nude.

To Do

for Joe Brainard

Never finish everything
on your to do list.

It will look as if you have nothing
better to do.

JOHN COLTRANE'S CENTRAL PARK WEST

Now this is the music
I imagine playing
if I were having an affair
with myself as a married man.

It's the music that would
always remind me
I always have me
in a special way
even if we aren't actually wed.

ASTOR PIAZZOLLA

Brujo, tell me the tragic
tall tales of the tango
according to your accordion.

Its fast and slow
jackrabbit crossbow—
deadweight glide.

Time isn't timid, you say,
so why should we be?

Sometimes I smell blood
in your cathedral.

Dismantled clock hands
move sensuously
up one another's
        downhill slide.

Defiant.
      Evasive.
You turn yourself in—

can't resist looking
wombward back.

A keyhole Orpheus.
A maudlin shape-shifting coat.

O how peculiar is
the perpendicularity of your song.

To know you is to be instantly elevated
to new depths.

Go on and lead then.
I'll follow your blizzard.

Sway on stiletto heels
through the winter's white heat.

GONE BUT NOT FORGIVEN

It's time to shake up that snow globe we call the world
and see what's happening in the near-far-middle-east-west.
I don't begrudge anyone the right to carry a grudge
through the purge of dark and bitter ages.
He should never have said that. She looked as if she meant.
They seemed to imply. It wasn't right and isn't.
Lately, something has turned up the volume on my volatility.
I was just looking for a moment of peace, but it made me
feel murderous. My counselor said: You are like really easy
to piss off. And then I wanted to kill him too!
He told me go and sit by a volcano and you will understand
each other. It's just that we all have so many grave insults
engraved upon us. I don't think it's fair for an enemy to die
and rob you of victory, go and leave you, fist still
shaking in the air—this isn't the end of this.

COMPETING LISTS

I have a long list of words
and when I fall asleep all the words
on my list will also be asleep
and able to be used in sleep.
But there is someone else
with an even longer list
whose job it is to make sure
everything stays awake.
After all, the world could end
accidentally if everything in it
went to sleep at the same time.
He's very serious and vigilant
about his job—drinking coffee
and taking speed—but I keep
adding more and more words
to mine, making it heavy and dreamy,
like loading cargo onto a boat.

WORD AND SENTENCE

lignify: v. To make woody or woodlike.

Daphne was lignified while fleeing Apollo.

The porn star could lignify himself at will.

siccative: n. A substance added to paints and some medicines to promote drying.

Quick, somebody throw the drowning man a siccative!

apiary: n. A place where bees are kept.

The happy couple spent their honeymoon in an apiary.

brattice: n. A partition, esp. one erected in a mine for ventilation.

Nothing is quite as cheery as a canary singing by a brattice.

flense: v. To strip the blubber or skin from (a whale, for example).

Serial killer, Ed Gein, once said he could outflense Melville in a second.

flexuous: adj. Bending or winding alternately from side to side.

Dualists claim the stairway to heaven is long and flexuous.

sastuga: n. A long wave-like ridge of snow found on the polar plains formed by wind.

Up past midnight, light writes upon the sastuga.

opuscule: n. A small and minor work.

You'd need a microscope to read his opuscule.

cresset: n. A metal cup suspended on a pole containing burning oil and used as a torch.

I got these cressets on sale at Crate & Barrel last week, along with some nice bamboo placemats.

rufescent: adj. Tinged with red.

After battle, the air glows rufescent with blood.

parasang: n. An ancient Persian unit of distance.

Wallace Stevens traversed parasangs on his way to the palace of the interior paramour, often going there straight from the insurance company.

utricle: n. A small, delicate membranous sac connecting the semi-circular canals of the inner ear and functioning in the maintenance of balance.

I tried but could not reach my utricles with a Q-Tip.

FOUND IN TRANSLATION

I've always liked reading poetry in translation. In fact, I prefer it that way.

Poetry is the sound one language makes when it escapes into another.

Whatever you think you've missed is, as the saying goes, better left to the imagination.

It gives even a mediocre poem an ineffable essence.

Greater involvement on the part of the reader leads to greater enjoyment.

A bad translation, a clumsy one, is especially charming.

The poem is whatever cannot be killed by the translator.

Its will to survive, its willingness to be uprooted and flee its homeland is admirable. I almost want to say virile.

An untranslated poem is too attached to its author. It's too raw.

An untranslatable poem that hordes its meaning, whose borders are too guarded, is better unsaid.

For years, I copied authors from around the world. Then one day it occurred to me, perhaps it's the translator I imitate, not the poet. This idea pleases me and makes me want to write more.

It would be great to learn French in order to read William Carlos Williams.

Translators are the true transcendentalists.

A Poetics of Optics

Pictures impregnate/
swallow us whole

like giants sleeping in gilded caves.

To them we're the artful ones—
moody: somehow false and somehow true.

The picture has its own way of looking,
though at times, it pretends not to see (us).

Hieroglyphics and holograms:
"Why you're nothing but a pack of cards!"

Coined signage.

Words and images are not opposed—
not goddess vs. machine.

Perhaps the poet is moved to write
by what Todorov calls
"the visual poverty of letters"

(as compared to painting).

We are poor; we must imagine.

Rimbaud binged on lavish spreads of hallucination.

Ponge spliced science and metaphor.

Williams has eaten the still life
and replaced it with an apology.

All images bank on alchemy,
though the Objectivists being materialists
called it history.

Symbols are meant to be clumsy.

Emanation isn't a one-way street.

Icons encourage us not to look *at them*—
wave us on to another world.

A Laminated Lament

for Philip Lamantia

Good grief! Pet sorrow!
Choked up mountains. Hiccuping hills.
Zoo of bygone instincts.
Lovers always leaping from the windows of their eyes.

Together the men, women, children—
all cry lustily, loudly,
their mouths full of candy,
for they know somewhere,
some tragedy is greater than their own,
some suffering outshines them.

With kittenish nerves,
with flat-topped frowns,
with cylinders of gloom
well-oiled in the garden of olives.

Alas and rejoice, for it has happened.
I've lost my sense of loss—
and now must go naked
without even a shadow
down the ancient street.

VAYA CON DIOS

You seem like
a nice enough deity,
but I'm not supposed
to talk to you anymore.

PERVERSELY PATRIOTIC

Terrorism has ruined
S & M for me.

Now it just seems
like watching
the news.

BAD FOLK SONG

It ain't bad
living in a
bad folk song.

The people
are friendly,

and the weather
is nice.

TWO DOZEN ROSES FOR
JACKSON MAC LOW: A CENTO

Beautiful roses of the past.
Sound rose. Dawn rose.
Blue rose kind of thing.
Take these roses climbing in the well of mirrors.
Know now that I am the roses
and it is of them I choose to speak.
The rose is out of town.
The rose is obsolete.
The general rose—decay.
My only rose tonight's the treat of my own nudity.
Roses hardy as clover return.
The militant roses.
The false roses—
the blood rose living in its smell.
Somewhere the sense makes copper roses,
steel roses. The rose carried weight of love.
The rose of paper is of the nature of its world
if roses would grow backwards.
Frail as April snow, the wrinkled roses tinkle.
Trees knit wind that roses tint with scent.
A little moth dressed in rose.
A large garden full of roses
and the villa there is one great rose.

THE FRAGRANCE GRIFTERS

sword
edged
flower

petal
soft
flame

*

wiggle
of girlie show

and arabesque

*

allergic
      counterpoint

*

fishnet of flight

*

the summer
summoned

leaf by leaf

*

infringing
on our darkness

*

bloodhound
      memory

*

playing
double-helix dutch
all day

UNISEX COLOGNES

AVATAR

There's one in each of us.

A barefoot prince
by a shoeless river.

GRASSHOPPER

Many varieties: veldt, pampas,
crab, Kentucky Blue, and more.

BLACK FOREST

Breezy. Bold.
Brooding. Bavarian.

Makes anytime
feel like the middle of the night.

ECHO

for Robert Creeley

It's all about
the lag time

between reflections
when Narcissus thinks:

it's my face,

only wetter,
maybe longer,

me but
not entirely—

something missing,
added?

I can't take my eyes
off it

(wait, are those my eyes?)

LEGACY

Now X is dead, so Y can be X.
And Z is dead, so A can be Z.
There's no shame in becoming someone else.
You may be even better at it than they were.
At times Z got in the way of our idea of him.
Before X was X, he was probably somebody else too.

ALMONDS

Almonds make me feel like autumn all year long. They're like a carrying case for tears that have dried but are still salty. When I'm gone, shed no almonds for me. The coffin-maker's daughter was an unusually happy child. She wanted only a pair of almond slippers to go clogging in—and a marzipan forest full of hand-painted leaves. Lorca was said to be able to play the almond and coax from it music to soothe melancholy moods. Instead of ice, Italians throw almonds at a bride and groom, perhaps because they think no pleasure complete without a bit of pain. In the palm of the hand, almonds nestle like pills said to transform phlegm, alleviate coughs, and soothe the intestines. Some worship the smooth lingam, but other secret societies extol the almond; pray daily to an edible rosary that they crunch between their teeth.

CIAO BELLA CHOCOLATE SORBET

has a dense
chewy

water-to-chocolate
ratio

as if a whole
devil's food cake

were dissolved
in each scoop.

Delivers Elvis-like
indulgence

for only 120 calories.
By the last spoonful,

your whole nervous system
and aura

will be permeated
by the ancient Mayan God.

You will see
through the eyes of Chocolate.

PRE-RAPHAELITE PINUPS

for Amy Gerstler

No one is saying how it came to be this way.
Sex is and is not part of the picture.

*

Too many people
wearing too many clothes,
thinking too few things.

*

The wallpaper is the real center of attention,
the figures mostly background music.

There is a rhythm to their eating.
One contemplates his wine,
another drinks it.

*

I never noticed it before
but that angel's feet are on fire!

*

It's a penitent's head
they've pasted on a voluptuous body.

*

Why, she's practically an insect herself.

*

Look how many worlds are woven
with the silly-string of the Fates.

*

The wheat field was like a drive-in movie
for the shepherd and his date.

*

The berry-boy offers his handful of red
to the gray little girl.

*

It's all in the fold,
the fertility dance of being draped over . . .

*

One could panel a library
with the grain of her hair.

*

Can't you see I'm just a poor,
blind, accordion-playing lesbian?

Do not disturb the visionary butterfly
at work in me.

*

The heretic wears a pretty demonic
apron and crown,

while Medusa's blue hairnet
tangles even the trees.

*

A squirrel, a robin;
an army of innocence
waits to molest a young girl—
asleep and unaware.

*

But isn't every story an allegory—
every house strewn with alchemical symbols like these?

*

Ach—but that rainbow is loud!
Too much beauty makes a person faint.

CONVERSATIONS WITH FOUNTAINS

for David Trinidad

While still a child
I discovered
the fountain of youth.

It kept me small
in all the right places,

insuring some part of me
would always be incompetent
and dependent,
impractical and silly.

Under its watery umbrella,
I stood spellbound for years,
trying to decipher its murmuring

and mimic the poses of pigeons
gathered round its basin,
one preening and one scholarly
and one flirtatious

like a cross section of society
from a Balzac novel—with wings!

Yes, part of the appeal of fountains
is how they make everything,
even water, seem to fly.

To be in love
is to speak and listen
to a fountain.

*

My mother had a mural
of a fountain sketched
on the living room wall
in charcoal and violet.

It was always dusk
no matter the time of day.

Our sofa curled beneath it,
a velvet cat, and I played
a chubby stick figure
in search of perspective,
lonesome as De Chirico.

Eventually we sold the house,
but the fountain did not disappear,
sprang up this time in the entrance
of my father's new Italian restaurant.

A statue taller than me
who poured water endlessly
from a stone jug.

Hebe, they called her,
goddess of youth,
companion of adolescents.

I worked as a hat-check girl
stationed opposite her;
the customers would throw us
each a coin.

Gradually, I came to see her
as a kind of stepmother, wise aunt.

Fountains, I realized, are thirsty too—
for company.

FOUNTAINS I'VE SAT BY:

Trafalgar Square, London

where I studied a map,
bronze lions looking over my shoulder,
as I tried to decide if there was time enough

to visit Freud's house,
see his collection of tchotchkes,
and get his blessing on ending my therapy.

As it turns out, there wasn't
and so I'm still talking.

After I finished with one analyst,
went on to another.

Just when you think you're done with the story,
the fountains says, "Go on."

Trevi Fountain, Rome

where Jean Peters, Dorothy McGuire,

and Maggie McNamara found love
to the memorable, if schmaltzy, theme song
sung by Frank Sinatra and written by Sammy Cahn.

There I made the necessary offering
with my mother, but so far have not returned.
Something about the place evaded me.

It's as if past and present are so intertwined,
they almost cancel each other out.

The city cannot be said to exist fully
in either dimension. Only the taste
of its hazelnut gelato proved eternal to me.

Buckingham Fountain, Chicago

It was a musical without need of music.

Arpeggios of spray crashing, floodlit,
then separating into juicy bands of fruited air—
droplets of lemon, lime, raspberry, grape.

Angelic Swedenborgian conversations
between gradations of light.

The ur-psychedelic experience before drugs.

Pretty but a bit over-the-top dramatic.
After a few minutes my attention would wander.

Give me a quiet, a shy fountain—
one content to sit in a small square gathering shade.

Washington Square, New York

If you must consult a liquid compass,
this isn't a bad one to keep in your back pocket.

Living around the corner from it, I feel its presence
even when I completely forget it's there,
look up and see its white plume wave a frothy hello.

There is something blatantly vagrant about it,
protective of free time and speech.
In an ultra-professional city like New York,
one could call it an amateur fountain,
a perpetual open mic.

Many times I've sat along its meridian
caught in the crossfire of klezmer and blues,
surprised by the variousness of the variety show
in the green room of the park.

It's a good place to practice being yourself,
or better still, put off that duty for another day.

Coda

Fabulous fountains of the future

Cooling whirlpool for funky feet

Photo op for minor actresses
looking to make a splash

To you I'll crawl
from the shipwreck of one moment
to the next

Oasis to oasis calling

(adult movie
late afternoon

    ghost ejaculating

        time loops back on

           the trees in black and white)

THE SHEEP OF DAYS

The calendar calls.

Without you
the seasons cannot change.

We will remain forever ramshackle,
forever pastoral even in the city,
forever eggs,
forever afternoon,
forever the murderous sweet nothings
of Scott Peterson and Amber Frey,
forever this humid humanity,
forever expressionless expressions
of love and disgust and distrust.

Dear days going and gone by—

We do not even mind so much
that you are numbered.

Like butter the sun melts
on your milky fleece.

Carpets flower beneath your hooves.

BENT ORBIT

I wind my way across a black donut hole
and space that clunks.
Once I saw on a stage,
as if at the bottom of a mineshaft,
the precise footwork
of some mechanical ballet.
It was like looking into the brain
of a cuckoo clock and it carried
some part of me away forever.
No one knows when they first see a thing,
how long its after-image will last.
Proust could stare at the symptom of a face
for years, while Frank O'Hara, like anyone with a job,
was always looking at his watch.
My favorite way of remembering is to forget.
Please start the record of the sea over again.
Call up a shadow below the pendulum of a gull's wing.
In a city of eight million sundials, nobody has any idea
how long a minute really is.

from

SURFACE TENSION

Tao

To go
round the world
with a flair
on a matchhead

from wharf
to ant farm

observing
all the signs
by rote

sad trot
charred nettles

the dog-eared webs
that hone the ether

until and then

furtive as a werewolf
you reappear
o path

INVOICE

Deliver boat
with mirrored oar
off Veneer Avenue.

Inflate dog.

Assemble teacup labyrinth.

Glue chair to wall.
Extend wall to accommodate
upscale sweep of eye
following curve.

Place egg
under pendulum timer.

Goldleaf ice.

Stuff pillows
in aquariums.

Fill coffins
with sand.

When guests arrive
ignore them.

A DATE WITH ROBBE-GRILLET

What I remember didn't happen.
Birds stuttering.
Torches huddled together.
The cafe empty, with no place to sit.

Birds stuttering.
On our ride in the country
the cafe empty, with no place to sit.
Your hair was like a doll's.

On our ride in the country
it was winter.
Your hair was like a doll's
and when we met it was as children.

It was winter
when it rained
and when we met it was as children.
You, for example, made a lovely girl.

When it rained
the sky turned the color of Pernod.
You, for example, made a lovely girl.
Birds strutted.

The sky turned the color of Pernod.
Within the forest
birds strutted
and we came upon a second forest

within the forest
identical to the first.
And we came upon a second forest
where I was alone

identical to the first
only smaller and without music
where I was alone
where I alone could tell the story.

MY ILLUSTRIOUS
GARGOYLE ANCESTORS

Blame it on genetics.

How one held a book
above a bakery.

How one was known
as the architect of love.

How one pointed the way to a dry cleaners
during the Renaissance.

Their grimaces flickering
above my crib.

The wordless shape
of things to come.

When I bit a tourist.
When I strangled a ballerina.

When I shut myself up in the vault.
Blame it on genetics.

A span as a gadabout
and then it was back to the slab

like a stone thrown through the centuries
that briefly mistakes itself for a bird.

FOLK DANCE

1. Carrying a tray.
2. Using a camera.
3. An undetermined celebration.
4. Up and down the stairs like
   the chambermaid in *The Dead*
   who says "men are all palaver
   and such as they can get."
5. Asparagus peeking out from
   under the salmon.
6. Coolness outside. Sky by Turner.
7. A square scarf folded to make
   a triangle.

MARIA CALLAS

Canaries faint
when caged
by the
metallic ardor
of your voice

filing its way
through the bars

as if
you intended
to pluck
the unfinished song

from their lungs
and devour it.

There is still
a touch of
the ancient myths

about you
though classically trained
as wild-eyed and tragic

to the opulence
of opera
you bring

a harsh
elemental reality:

vinegar stored
in an oak casket,

salt poured
on an enemy's wounds.

ANOTHER FORM OF
SUICIDAL BEHAVIOR

Even in this heat
they won't stop wearing all black

leather and mascara.
God it must be awful

like being a nun
in the old days.

I used to love watching nuns sweat
but these kids really suffer

and pay a high price for having watched
too many episodes of *The Munsters*.

Some will certainly collapse
before they even reach

the Chinese restaurant
on the corner

and one has the distinct impression
that those who do survive

will never look
totally cool again.

LESBIAN CORN

In summer
I strip away
your pale kimono.
Your tousled hair too,
comes off in my hands
leaving you
completely naked.
All ears and
tiny yellow teeth.

APPROACHING ORGASM

Under a green bough
                    history expires.
As into the well I dive
                    knowing well
that I shall return empty-handed
or clutching only the ragged outline
                    of you and you.
Dear me,
but in summer a great horniness
overwhelms us like a tidal wave
                    of sleep.
Outside and in, everything is blurred,
fuzzy, partially melted.
I am buying peaches
and I have a great desire
                    to eat one
flaunting its curve in the market.
Also today I went to the library
but it feels as though I'm returning
from a much longer journey
                    perhaps
all the way back from the Nile.
Since my eyes are closed
much of the time, I can't be sure,
still it seems Cleopatra's voice
was calling me
                    as with a thud
workmen dropped the walls back in place.
Strange isn't it,
how views change
and now I approach orgasm

like one taking a day off.
It is simply blank space
                              on the calendar
but of course, in other cultures
it means something else
and must be approached
in an entirely different way.

MARTHA GRAHAM

1.
In 1923
for the Greenwich
Village Follies

you performed
three dances
one Oriental
one Moorish

and one
with a large veil.

You said:
"Grace is your
relationship
to the world"

a deep-rooted
inclination
to converse

and just as poetry
is not about words
nor math about numbers

so too the dance
is not about its steps.

2.
With your spooky
Franz Kline makeup
and adolescence
of Indian maidens

the daughter
of Dr. George Graham
a specialist
in nervous disease

you dance
not with lyrical hands
but with the nervous system

capricious and sterile
as a guillotine for swans

dark fins
circling the white
of the eyeball.

CRUSADE

At some point
while still living
here
I had already
moved away
and begun
growing up
on nothing but

the novocaine
of pure adventure.

A spiky planet

where I knew
many fewer words

those small
wildflowers

       white and red

not even their names.

AT THE END OF SUMMER

for Louis Zukofsky

Go on
Mr. Tree Fugue
I'm listening.

AT THE MALL

They
do the gathering
for us
       take it all in
and give back
choices
       however limited.
They keep it together
       music   art
knows its place
in the system.
Money is refreshing
and the salespeople
       seem genuinely concerned
not so much
about music   art
or us
but about continuity
or maybe harmony
the shape
       that each transaction
takes in the larger context
of the day
as in
       "have a good one"
endlessly chanted mantra
to the patron saint of cash flow.

CRICKETS CRUSH WOMAN

Can't shake
the "I'm next" feeling.

Attuned to memory
and the redundancy
of the power system
it sets up.

Body seems slower,
            more withdrawn.

Each time you return
and find it slightly altered

when you
just want
to relax.

Pornography
but with the good parts
missing.

On a Saturday night
you should always
buy yourself something.

In the past
it would have been
a drink

but now
the old songs
sound terrible.

Clothes are
either too light
or too dark.

In a Monotonous Dream

The language
created the landscape

and there was only
one word

which meant
at various times

depending on
the inflection

motherdeath
cabbagefangs

ominous headwaiter
sinister whirring

bad joke
rude uncle

song that is stuck
half-open window

lecturing priest and
bride that was never a virgin.

PURITANS

There are no small ones.
All big-boned

men and women
without a hint of child's play.

They creak
as they walk

like doors left open
to bang in the wind.

One imagines from their gait
that years from now

they will make androit bowlers.
Meanwhile, they whisper

careful not to sound rhythmic.
Dovegray, lavender, and eggshell

are the only colors
and even these must be bleached, muted

in order for their profiles
to emerge on cold cash

as if doodled there
with invisible ink.

If not optimistic,
they are eternally democratic

and can be handled
without contamination.

That word
has no meaning for them.

Touch them
as much as you like,

wherever you please.
They have never felt

the desire to reciprocate
and for that they are grateful.

BEING SICK TOGETHER

In the postmodern world
the sequel is always superior

to the original
and it is even possible

for someone like Tony Perkins
to meet a nice girl in *Psycho III*

a suicidal former nun
who is also tormented

by sexual fantasies
so that he can teach her something

old-fashioned as dancing
the fox trot

and she can offer him
a drink in her room.

At the Bates Motel
water drawn from the same tap

where famous shower scene began
now seems pleasantly refreshing.

Surface Tension

1.
that feeling
of resignation
that comes
            before change

2.
someone calls
and says
she has seen a body
flying through the air

maybe now
isn't a good time
to talk

3.
fuck shapes

4.
replace the narrative
with another
form of narrative

5.
aping
the lush life

6.
the Hansel and Gretel
basement

the endless supply
of cookies

7.
the rarely seen
pistachio green

8.
privacy

9.
as another form of intimacy

10.
they call that
        a sucker punch

11.
when a woman
walks toward you

the way she did

something happens

12.
it's like mailing a letter

13.
you think of things
as coordinates

14.
you replace sleep
with pointing

THE FOREIGN LEGION

It's pleasant
to wake
to a camel's nuzzling
even on the run.
Glorious,
not to give a hoot
about anything
and say so
but best of all
is the exotic way
everything normal
begins looking
in order to
win you back.
How the moment
in need
of being rescued
turns its helpless eye
toward you
as you
draw your sword,
reckless and lonesome.

AFTER A PROMISING YOUTH

Once on vacation
he threw the pyramids
a curveball
and ever since
it's been hopeless.
Now a dishwasher
he works
in a Tarot Card
above the city.
Cooped up all day
in the fairy-tale sky,
evenings he sings dirges.
Weekends he likes to be
tied up and whipped.

THINGS TO DO IN THE BIBLE

Get drunk.
Walk on water.
Collect foreskins.
Pluck out an eye.

Build an ark.
Interpret dreams.
Kill your brother.
Don't look back.

Join a tribe.
Listen to clouds.
Live in a tent.
Quit your job.

Take to the hills.
Report to the king.
Raise the dead.
Seek the spirit.

Reap what you sow.
Count your blessings.
Gnash your teeth.
Fish for men.

Grow a beard.
Wear a cowl.
Ride a donkey.
Carry a torch.

Sit by a well.
Live to a ripe, old age.
Remain a virgin
and speak in tongues.

These are the words of the Lord.

BREAKFAST WITH JEROME

Light shivering on its tightrope

Bizet in the background

Banana bread and a pear

Swinging its lantern of white noise

The chef's hat perches on the fence

The coachman is driving the city to the city

Magically the page refills itself

You Go to My Head

The outcome was
unexpected
          a light silly note
          on the table
after rowing like a galley slave
to open the bronze door
          and still in my
"journey to the center of the earth"
          rags,
I come home to find
such music as I've never heard pour
from the dolphin-headed faucets.
It's just that I had pictured
something more dramatic
          than a cocktail.
Who thinks of such things
          in a gloomy old cave?
"But my dear," you said
winding a towel around your head,
"it doesn't take a genie
to see you're destined
          for fun,
and awful as it sounds
you must learn to make the best of it."

ESCAPE FROM WOMEN'S PRISON

1.
We had almost forgotten what men were,
the part they played in our downfall.
On our breaks in the yard
where the air smelled of shampoo
we thought of ourselves as almost good
and it was only occasionally
that one or the other
heard a voice from outside call.
"There was plenty of dope in Florida," Annie'd say,
"and we smoked it all in convertible cars and Holiday Inns."
Then she'd stop, like she was trying to picture something
and each time she told it, the story got shorter.
It was the same for everybody.
In the heat of the workroom,
we'd hallucinate zippers,
but when their clothes fell away,
there was only the long rows of washboards.
"If ever there were men on this planet," Iris mumbled,
"they existed a long time ago."

2.
Another time the warden
sent us out to pick strawberries, two by two.
"Are you thinking about men?"
We were on our backs in this field.
The plants were real short
so we had to lay down if we wanted any shade.
I was thinking about church.
"Jesus was a man," I said.
"Yeah, but not the one I'm thinking of. This one

had eyes that were always chatting."

"Do you think they watch? Sometimes I get the feeling that the whole prison is surrounded by men. Sometimes I get the feeling all we'd have to do is ask and they'd take us anyplace we wanted to go."

ALEISTER CROWLEY SLEPT HERE

There is something banal about evil
but the reverse is also true
and what is mundane quickly becomes sinister.
Like the building on the corner
where his ghost tampers with a geranium.
So ordinary yet gloomy,
one senses he was bored
and this can be verified
in his autobiography, wherein he states,
"I confess to dislike Chicago . . .
It gives the impression of being a pure machine."
Of his apartment, there is not much to see.
A Weber grill, pale yellow and never used
that the new tenants installed on the balcony.
If I meet them, I will ask
if they have nightmares often
although it is not likely.
He was older when he resided here.
Pretty much the retired Prospero
who'd broken his wand in favor of literature.
A mistake, in this city, as he found out
when calling on the editor of *Poetry* magazine.
A poetess, of whom he writes,
"I am still not sure if she knew my name
and my work, but she showed no interest whatsoever!"
As you see, things haven't changed.
I live down the street
and often he haunts the neighborhood
searching, as I am, for this or that line.
And after storms I always think
those knots of wet string

you find coiled on the sidewalk
must surely have belonged to him.

A BOUQUET OF OBJECTS

Lovely to be
like a racehorse surrounded by flowers

but it is also lovely
to be surrounded by air and own pendants

and bracelets of soot.
Here is a factory made fresh by broken windows

and there is my muse
returning home with a pail of milk.

He brings me
down to earth where all poetry begins

with such beautiful hands
that I am forever doing nothing but thinking

of objects
and asking him to hold them.

PALE YELLOW

Of course I
want your approval
               desperately

as I want
a second cup
               of coffee.

The morning slips
out of its tee shirt.
               A chill,

pale yellow
big bunch of lilies
               billowing

holds my attention
in mid, not flight,
               so much as upward clamor.

Reflections of a vaguely
southwestern "el Navajo
               fire-escape" pattern

paint the window
across the street.
               I want to lick them off.

FOR DAVID HOCKNEY

Cock sweet.
Wind studied.
Housework
complete.
Pool lacquered
like a Turkish
cigarette case.
Nice light.
Book in bed.
The hours strike
sotto voce.

from

DECOY

BRAND X

I know you think
this is about sex
but that's only because
it's really about advertising.

Someone talking
in an office.
Someone comparing two things.

I make decisions
or my body
makes them for me
and certain nights
everything is perfect.

Wedges of light flap
slow as Indian summer.
A red receding.

There is real violence
but it's an after-dinner violence
mellow in the air
as sex is a kind of violence

like anything
that pulls us toward it
even though we're unable
to ask for it by name.

MEN IN CAMISOLES

All writing is a form
of transvestism.

Men in camisoles.
Women drinking port
and smoking thin cigars.

Think of Flaubert, Proust,
Mallermé in drag.

Or a woman (any woman)
trying on a man's power:
"Now I clothe myself
in your blood, your wars."

Like getting dressed
in a warm room
on a cold day

the sly smile
of the self
as it goes to sleep.

Everything contained within.
You read Rilke
and you become Rilke.

Nothing can stop this
endless, transformative
flow of selves
into other, opposite,
even objects and animals.

In a dream I took my
blue pentagram shirt
to the cleaners

and they said
it would take
three whole months
to get the werewolf out!

Dear Michael

The real
is looser
than the hyper-real

and I'm glad
after all these years
to tell them apart.

Fairfield Porter says:
"I don't paint space,
I paint the air"

and I say
I don't look at color
(at least in your backyard)
I breathe it.

Not that you
remind me of Fairfield Porter
(to bring up class!)

it's just that
I was so happy
to be in your guest room
reading Barbara Guest

with "real" bluebirds outside
and Hank Williams warbling
in the next room.

Domesticity,
that's what my dream
was about

as in: where's the tea,
the cups, the sign
over the sink that reads

"There is a silent
meaning behind everything"

(like a monastery)

and when people ask
we tell them that you're
going through a Thomas Merton phase

but still like to party
on weekends.

In the Mail Today

1.

A reminder
that my student loan
is overdue.

Amazing, this debt
from another life
when I waitressed
and read 19th-century novels.

First the French.
Then the British.

Now, forty
and still paying.

2.

A long letter
from a new friend
in Minnesota
where it's even colder
than it is here—
2 below to our 18 degrees.

It ends:

I feel almost
as if I should
apologize

for dumping

all these words
on you.

Strange—
we speak this way,
humans do,
so seldom now
that it almost seems
on the outside.

3.

A postcard
from Joe Brainard.

Dear Elaine and Jerome,
        Don't miss Ruby Stone's
(she's a he) cooking show
Come and Get It on Saturdays
at 1:00 P.M. on channel 17.

4.

An envelope
from St. Anthony's
(patron of lost things)
Church.

Ornately addressed
to me but with
nothing inside,

the message
apparently forgotten
or misplaced.

AFTER HERRICK

true calendars
tell ripe
each change

assuage
as night does

doting
and yet shines

enclosed in
rhymes
sphering

Bestrewed
with Ovid
(bellman Ovid)

words
for meat
give melody
over rocks

reading
by degrees

rivers
turn awhile
to men

awhile
they glide
full of meaning

shearing
melody's
meeting

DESTINATIONS

1.

A hand
leafs through
autumn

with a logic
that shines
like oxblood.

Every morning
I don't hear it

the absence
behind the bird.

Nudging the frame.
Singing its head off.

2.

Your letter
is full of energy

as though you were
inside a color
a whole flock of them

but I slept
on the day
I was born

and see sleep
as others see the world.

A lamp filled with
the oil of dreams

hisses, stone chatter.

3.

In brine daylight
thought becomes brimmed.
Fraught with sudden,
steeped in listening.

The jars
around which presence
gathers its virtues.

To inhabit my walk
(though a pleasure)
and all that that conveys

(limitations, frames).

This romance
of going from city to city
with a lamp.

ART ABOUT FEAR

1.

Be careful with that book.
It's not a book. It's a person

and it changes. See, there's lavender
under the frost. And an accident.

Grow up and decide for yourself
what it's about, but it's too bad

it can't be me because I'm very good
if you're terrified. That's what I do.

Art about fear. Girls that burst
into flames while getting a suntan.

2.

Text
is something
we all must
share

the burden of
carrying.

Rub shoulders with
and give it a push.

Evening's door
swings open
and there you are
in my skyline
with the peek-a-boo crotch.

Body dimensions sweep.
I'm sweeping.

Wrong in this context
but I can imagine another
where suppose . . .

3.

His offering me a cigarette
only seemed to underscore
the close-but-no-cigar bit.

When I perceive an obstacle
I feel it physically.
How approach? How get past?

Its looming legend.
Pepper trees that can walk
two full miles per day.

The question isn't
whether it's true or not
but whether you *want* to believe it.

4.

Some objects
are like a sieve
that language
passes through
while others
repel the alphabet
with a harsh
clanging skin.
Minor intelligences
perched on
the tip of.
Go ahead, say it
in your Bullwinkle French.

5.

You know classical perspective doesn't really
exist, but off in your vortex, it sounds roman-
tic. Seeping through those flickering inhibitions
that lead back home to maroon with its old-
fashioned horror. Like hair standing on end,
the water shot straight up out of the fountain.
This was my first painting. The portrait of a
lonely, intrepid rationalist besieged by spirits.

6.

Eventually meaning
does arrive.
The latecomer
with a festive air.

As if to say:
"There are paintings.
There are books, but nothing
here to frighten you."

Then suddenly
and for no reason
it disappears again.

What recourse
against such loss
but to make a list.

Say prayers.
Wash clothes.
Buy groceries.
Call David.

7.

After the funeral
we threw open the windows.

Cooling there.
Words,
loaves of them.

Such a lonely sound.
A carriage
(in these modern times)
passing below.

With Rimbaud
and his mistress
stuck inside.

Still searching
for that spider
that goes so fast
and travels far.

Its poisonous scratches
like those of a pen.

UP THE LADDER OF ENLIGHTENMENT

"I've just gotten
to the point where
I can deal with roaches

but mice—

mice are still
beyond me."

My Father Sees a UFO

He sits between the phone and the refrigerator.
While behind him, the trees outside the window
are caked with snow. Everything is silent, but
at a slightly different pitch, and he sits like
one lost in the Bermuda Triangle of their various
stillnesses. To his right is a glass of vodka.
To his left, hovering just above the shoulder,
is a large mysterious ball of light. Clearly,
it frightens him, but still he looks, with eyes
that are both liquid and resigned, as if he
always expected this to happen. Months
earlier, his wife asked for a divorce.
Months later will find him in the hospital
after a stroke. Yet at just this moment, nothing
seems to matter except that he listen to whatever
has traveled light-years to reach him—a sound
small as the ice melting in his glass.

Ninety Percent of
All Serial Killers

have three things in common: bedwetting
past the age of twelve, several episodes
of starting fires, torturing animals.
When I close my eyes at the end of the day,
this is all that comes to mind. After washing
dishes, grading papers, writing letters, long
conversations on the phone and in restaurants,
time spent memorizing Italian verbs: *cogliere*
to gather, *accendere* to light—nothing else
it turns out is quite so memorable to me as this.
The sort of thing you hear once and, for some reason,
take it with to your grave. Strange, how we mark
our place in the world.

MULBERRY STREET

It's the kind of street
that would be behind
one of those crooners
who sang on TV in the 1950s.

A streetlamp, a cemetery
and a big full moon.
What more could a person
want or need?

O to live on nothing
but arugula and espresso,
forever doing penance
in that somber church
across the street.

The one that's surrounded
by a wall that leans on you
as much as you lean on it.

The one full of flickering lights
and statues that talk.
"The dead," they say.
"The dead will outlive us all."

PRESCRIPTION

Take Herrick
for melancholy

Niedecker
for clarity

O'Hara
for nerve

A LEMON

In the lemon
we find a fire
that cools, coos.
Mathematically succinct
it is a flame
which unlike most
can be cut in half
or thirds if you prefer.
In the skin
of its lantern
light implodes,
slowing to the speed
of mere human endeavor
before giving itself
in a last sudden burst
like eyesight
to the blindness
of the mouth.

DECOY

violins
scissor a tune
streaked with animal

not what I want to be
but where I am

(makes the connection)

oh yes, now I recognize it

vigilantly
mapped out

facts awaken
almost by touch

a shape
unseen
yet so familiar

*

there was an old uncle vampire
giving his niece a drink

but it was the shabbiness
of where it took place
(not in a Gothic drawing room)
that upset us

*

think of ready-ing
as doing the prerequisite reading

clouds slide
smoothly over the skin

"He lives in his legend
and that's about it"

a neatly folded labyrinth

going by:
blue blooms on the red field
of a dress in motion

if only we could get
that feeling back where
it's the landscape that moves
and the viewer who stands still

"Yes, yes
we have to get together

and no, I don't
remember who you are."

*

somewhere behind eye and ear
coffee is brewing, bread baking

the sign reads:
"Looks are deceiving
it's eating
that is believing—

mind crawls like a fly
over the painted fruit

form struggles
not only to emerge
but also to sink
back into matter

these flowers
smell more dead
than alive

so where does the mania
for containment come from?

*

historically the doppelgänger
is not a nice person

bone prism casts
body-stocking shadows

see Artaud in the role
of game-show host

or *Let's Make a Deal*
as theater of cruelty

flames nest
doubling back

dissolves into unrest
and needless hyperbole

an impersonation
pressing down on

*

UFO SLICES HOTEL
CAKE WITH FIRE ESCAPE ICING

willow seen by candlelight
poems read by flashlight

    sage
    marigolds
    Salems
    Rolling Rock

"You're going to hell
in a handbasket with the rest of us"

*

stains:
what works on paper
doesn't always

and that's the story of my life

biting through
glimpses

an exchange of parcel,
password, fishbowl, globe

"Most normal people are sick"

until at some point
evil stops being evil
and just stands childishly
under the childish stars

AFTER BACON

to know the names
of all the muses, planets, plants
(everything that ever existed)

unpronounceable
faded and obscure
Greek and Latin names

and to still find
in this world

a place for them
        to mate
            match with . . .

like a Cinderella
who is herself
made of glass

o empiricism
o anatomy

AH!

How good it feels
even briefly
to stretch
the long neck
of narcissism.
One happiest
blue-checkered tablecloth
of infinite seeing
eye to I.
And with love's mask
in place
what world lies
behind the curtain?
In Rome, it's true
there is no Rome
but elsewhere—plenty.

To Harry Crosby at the Hotel Des Artistes

In 1979, on the 50th anniversary of your
double-suicide, I came like a bridesmaid
dressed in black to scatter rose petals
in the lobby. Then I went home and listened
to Joy Division, whose lead singer would
also kill himself. Death was everywhere
at the time, though mostly as a fashion
statement—kohl around the eyes and
safety pins through the cheek—with
the real devastation still to come. Now it
is 1993 and no one much likes to glamorize
their death wish, not since AIDS has made
absence so conspicuous. Today people prefer
to look healthy, and it's mineral water I
toast you with in the Art Deco jungle of the
hotel bar. Not the sort of place I'd choose
if I were going to end it all, but if I've
become anything, I hope it's more tolerant—
even of the very rich. Outside on the ground
there is no snow yet, but old rice the color
of ivory, leftover from some other wedding,
and in the bare trees, white lights like a
handful of rice, transformed on this winter
afternoon into "the pleasure of neon in daylight."
Perfect moments in an imperfect world, joined
together so that even death cannot separate them.

SOMETIMES I GET DISTRACTED

for Philip Whalen

Throwing a ball

like a bridge
over an old wound

like a cape
thrown chivalrously
over incoherent muck.

Catching it
is easy.

"Now toss it back,"

says the Zen monk
standing in his garden
centuries away.

from

VOICE-OVER

DETAIL

Not the mansion
but the gate.

Not the cloth
but the crease.

Not the face
but the nose.

Not the speech
but the tone.

Not the pomegranate
but the seeds.

Not the nest
but the egg.

Not Ophelia
but her bouquet.

Not the torso
but the arm.

Not the ship
but its sail.

Not Courbet
but his dog.

Not all of Kerouac
but certainly parts.

Not *Madame Bovary*
as a whole

but as a collection
of individual details

textures, perfumes
that the mind carries off

one at a time.
And always, always

there is the eye
separating, isolating

calculating difference
like profit and loss.

Self Portrait as You

Always receding
you are
what I come out
to see.

You
      "multi-you"

who shuffles the cards,
who never comes forward
but simply appears

on a roller coaster
or looking at the waves—

the static poses
in which I multiply myself.
In a sense you are
what happens to me,

speaking through events
or when you choose

through aura's last residue
of touch—

the product that says "buy me,"
the object that glows.

When I understand
I see

and when I am tired
or confused, I have
nothing to show

that sliver of the whole
that is just you being you—

a new moon which grows the old
again and again, but different
each time. Tonight's heavy as
an enormous peach

drooping over a side street.
The light a fragrant slant
that lingers through next day

changing
as you yourself shift

from lover
to father or mother,

from singer
to silence,
then back to song.

In you
I view myself
at a distance

yet from there
you always seem
more real than me

more able to move
or think or speak

while I can only
write you off,

dreaming of a conversation
where voices don't match faces—
Heidegger's words
in Marilyn Monroe's mouth.

Today seventy percent
of the population believes
in angels, but I don't think
of you in such sentimental terms.

except at times
you seem like a woman,
at times a man.

Impossible to determine
sex, age, race, height—

the answer enfolded,
enveloped somewhere out there
in the head-over-heels blue.

What is the sky anyway,
but a reply to the earth.

PINK SHUTTERS

for David Trinidad

Pink Shutters—Pink Shutters!
Sixty-three pairs opened wide
in the narrow alley

as if Mao had once again proclaimed
"Let a hundred windows bloom"
—kiss by kiss.

Shocking Pink! Pagan Pink!
Milk of Magnesia and Panther Pink
seductively pulling us into the air

like a harem of wings
in which we desire and are perhaps afraid
to be lost forever.

We who have just left jobs,
families, packages below
while the eye continues to climb—

refuses, in fact, to come down from
this giddy Jacob's Ladder of Wild Pinks,
Wild Pinks ascending!

THESIS SENTENCE

Elaine moves a step forward
and everyone else goes back to work.

All day the curtains are moved by the breeze
and some say it is a sign from God.

X writes as if she were God
and knows what it's like to be God all the time.

Others say God is a set of words
held tightly together by an invisible bond—

not one can be added or removed.
The poem is a small machine made of God.

BEAUTY SECRET

The beautiful
and the hideous

often conspire
in an empire
of appearance.

So which side
would you rather be on—

or NEITHER

like the one
hurrying by,
eyes averted,

arms full of packages:

"These are necessities
not beauty aids.

Excuse me and
thank you very much."

*

It must be
like losing your
fear of death

to just stop
worrying about
what you look like—

no longer tied
to that lamppost

like a dog
in the rain.

*

From my mother
I learned to fear beauty,
the lack of it

and from my father
to distrust it.

Like eyes,

the heart too
turns away

sets its sights
elsewhere.

*

If only people aspired
to the charm
of odd things:

miniature golf courses
or buildings
in a certain light

but, of course,
they don't.

*

The sun sets.
The vase rests
in the center
of the poem.

It is all
a matter of arrangement.

Relationships
of power

made to seem
natural
and right.

MONOLOGUE: FRANK O'HARA

Untie your muse
for an hour and stay with me.

I come in pieces
across a great test pattern

or maybe it's what I used to call sky.
The music is certainly blue enough

but not without its own tenderness
like an arrow shot I know not where.

When will you see me as I am
as industrious with grief as you are

clever at hiding your tiredness.
In poems we shine,

and though we say them with conviction,
the words are never really ours for keeps.

TABLE OF CONTENTS FOR AN IMAGINARY BOOK

Spree
Monster Gardens
Up Close, Out Back, Down Under
Flying Backward
The Drunken Voluptuary Workers in the Solarium
Dove Sighting
All The Yellow in the World
A Curse I Put on Myself
Three Sides of the Same Coin
Aria
Night Cream
Good Luck With Your Chaos
The Glass Stagecoach
In the Country of Mauve
Parrots and Dictators
Slumming
Walking the Evening Back Home
A Twelve Course Dinner of Regret
The Gap Gatherer
Burning Down the Ocean
Multiple Choice

SECOND THOUGHTS

for Rae Armantrout

1. Once one has learned the trick of keeping up appearances—it's very hard to get beyond that.

2. To vegetate: from the Latin *vegetare* meaning to enliven.

3. Androgynous-looking men and women always look androgynous in the same way—as if there was a right and wrong way to do it.

4. Speaking a language is different from feeling it. One Japanese woman says that when she swears in English, she feels nothing.

5. Doesn't it seem wonderfully optimistic when someone you hardly know signs a note "Love"? And, in fact, doesn't it make you love them just a little for doing it?

6. The light shines on the lavender, but the effect is one of their being illuminated from within—as if the external light only drew our attention to the inner light that is theirs alone.

7. Bedded down like a mollusk.

8. Unlikely heroes: Fate in the musical comedies of the 50s. Time in the new novel of the 60s. Language in the critical thinking of the 70s.

9. Where would I like to die? In a bakery, I think—as in one of those religions where the corpse is surrounded by sweets and fruit.

10. Not every stone that's been rejected by the builder can become the cornerstone—just one of them.

11. The sunflowers are the table's antennae.

12. There are women who begin cleaning, then discover that they can't stop. It's the housewife's version of *The Red Shoes* and it really does happen.

13. My greed is never so apparent as when I pray—yet isn't it also a sign of faith?

14. Like any relationship, a new sex fantasy needs to be carefully cultivated. Some you may entertain only briefly, but others can last a lifetime.

15. Sexual fantasies are more than just mood music.

16. Her objects were arranged on the shelf like a sentence

beginning with an Aztec sacrificial knife and ending with the photograph of an old woman.

17. My father had a genius for appreciating kitsch, and his talent always made me feel like there were depths I would never be able to sink to.

18. On being moved by a will other than one's own: she said her journal was living her life for her; she said she had begun to feel like she was her cat's pet!

19. What speech shares with birds: both live in the air.

20. Confidence comes from knowing you can always get back what you lose.

21. Messiah Complex: One at a time, imagine everyone you know as dead; then, one at a time, bring them back to life again.

22. What It Amounts To: One particularly vivid childhood memory I have is of literally standing on a hill of beans. A six or seven foot hill—which given the neighborhood I grew up in seems highly unlikely. Nevertheless . . .

23. To muse: from the Latin *mus* meaning snout!

24. To be understood, cliches are as necessary as syntax or grammar.

25. Every day I discover more and more products I can't live without.

26. Do men find themselves talking in a voice that is not quite their own—slightly higher, lower, younger—as often as women do?

27. All voices have a tactile quality and are meant to be felt as well as heard.

28. There are people who look out the window to see the future—its arrival.

29. Even a landscape can make a gesture toward us.

ARMANI WEATHER

In that long
navy blue
cashmere coat,
he was made
to do nothing
but lean against
tall buildings.
A somber
exclamation point,
eating an apple—
turning it slowly
into ballet.
How extravagant
yet restrained,
the way he wears
the space
around his body
loosely.
Even the light matches,
pale and cold
and slightly green,
like the apple
against his dark skin.

Remorse After Shopping

Why did I buy it?
What was I thinking?
It's all wrong.
Tacky, but not in a good way.
It looks suburban.
It spells housewife.
Too nurturing.
I don't even have kids.
No one will take me seriously.
It must have been the lighting.
I was in a hurry.
I don't even want to return it.
Just get it out of here.
Throw it away.

WANG WEI'S MOON

for David Shapiro

Leisurely
it comes out—

new moon
like the eyebrow
of a moth,

full moon
that burns
the pines,

or suddenly
         sad

remote
above a gate,

or glaring
         clarity

like a lamp
that quiets windows.

Cold
it tumbles into
random shadows

alarming birds,

              far far
stone cliffs
shine

as someone
washes silk
in moonlight.

Unsteady images
tied to whiteness.

Stars
float up
toward dawn.

ALMOST TRANSPARENT

for Lorine Niedecker

You and your books:

>   quotes
>   fly overhead
>   like clouds

Your words:

>   quick and
>   emerald green

>   chameleon-like
>   in the spic and span
>   kitchen

You think you've disappeared—

Stoic:

>   a Garbo
>   of the Midwest,

>   a swamp queen

>   Ms. Dickinson
>   comes visit
>   Mr. Basho
>   comes for tea

You *think* you're part of the landscape

      soaked-in
      water-voiced

but it's you I see moving (isn't it?)

      behind the sheer
      almost transparent curtain
      of your poems

CUPBOARD/SHRINE

If I have
an image of mind

it's as
general store:

boxes and
canned goods

to be moved
and dusted behind.

The idea
and its opposite,

paint and turpentine,
side by side—

honey and vinegar
on the shelf below.

FROM LORINE

How am I really?
I'm all right.
I enjoy my home,
even myself sometimes.
Enmeshed in nuisances
of course but no real troubles.
How are you really?

*

Hair almost all gray now?

Eyebrows are the last
to show age and eyes never.

*

The world is busy
rushing past my door . . .

life is weeds
instead of grass—
not even weeds
but water.

*

Don't send Xmas present—

I have something for you
not at all expensive either.

So just draw a picture
of a pine tree

which is one kind of tree
I don't have.

*

Last night
it rained here. Everything
has decided to live.

Luffly
            little dellycut moments

strings of geese
going over
            and spiders
            starting to crawl.

It has been hard
to sell magic—
will the time come
when it can't
be *given* away?

FENNEL

for Melanie Neilson

What is there is say about fennel—with its heavy
licorice tongue that makes one feel both drowsy and
wide awake? Whole it looks remarkably like a hookah
or else a bottle of eau de cologne. And the taste
is like that too. A sort of cigarette and breath
mint swallowed all in one bite. Cut into, its flesh
unwinds like a roll of film—shot half in winter,
half in spring. As much a liqueur as fruit or
vegetable. As much a beginning as an end.

STARTING TO RAIN

for Joe Brainard

Distracted, I leave
the therapist's office
but even walking fast
they catch my eye

make me stop
and look

while they look back.

Dark and light
blue pansies
in a white window box.

So small—

how did they manage
to make themselves heard?

LETTER OF RECOMMENDATION

Please say something really good,
no, *great* about yourself. I would
but I am watching a porno movie
and have no time to write.
The woman astride the man is a ghost
and the fact that she's dead
makes it seem more artistic.
I'm afraid I'll be busy for months.
You know I love your work,
think highly of you—
but then these ghosts arrive
and somehow a person can't say no.
They are so demanding.
To get away even for coffee
seems a lot. It's difficult
to know where it will end,
especially when he doesn't suspect
the ghost is really a brunette actress
in a blonde wig. She says
part of him wants to be fooled.
Meanwhile, remember how brave
and talented you are.
I would add beautiful too
but that might sound strange.
So just write anything,
something glowing—
and sign my name.

VOICE-OVER

1.
Climbing the Tower of Babel
we ascend into noise,

every sort of hybrid—
pig squeals grafted onto wheels

burning rubber.
But coming down, dissonance fades

and contradictions fold
into a single voice.

Reassuringly direct, it says:
"Psychic advisors are waiting."

It says: "Perfection is coming."
It says: "Call now for free samples."

It says: "Week after week, we tackle
the questions you'd like to ask God."

2.
Once upon a time,
far away, in a booth
of glass and light

a man cleared his throat
and a woman adjusted her headphones
in order to send their breath—

just the sound of it—

like bees
to circle and inflate
all things hollow,

sculpting the air itself
into a story
we soon came to think of as ours.

This narrow world,
a silent movie,
longs for those voices

on high to float down
with their sprigs of color,
canned laughter,

their rational explanations
lovingly applied.

3.
Disembodied
the voice
conveys
intimacy
(even personality)
but at a distance.
Thus we are
less judgmental,
more willing
to listen
and eager to buy.
In poetry too
we like our lyricism
minus the garlic
on the poet's breath.

4.
Here is stock footage of clouds
followed by mudslides, earthquakes, monsoons—

a time-lapse change of seasons
over which the narrator says:
"We've come through it all and so can you."

Don't worry.
Here is a gloved hand, a pair of scissors,
a paper heart.

Don't worry.
"Make yourself in as passive,
or receptive a state of mind as you can."

(Almost as if you were taking dictation.)
"Put your trust in the inexhaustible
nature of the murmur."

Don't worry.
Voice imposes order. From above.
Someone else's voice.

Using violence first and then seduction
or vice-versa.

The mother's and then the father's voice.
The neutral voice of science
familiar as a lullaby.

5.
How like
an ear
the earth

listens,
lies down
to listen—

a spoonful
of sounds
dissolving

in the dream
where mouths move
out of sync.

6.
Scripted,
it is not natural.

It only appears that way
to sell the Grecian urn
or Grecian Formula 44—

the death in the family
like a used car.

And yet
we do hear them,

these voices.

Like St. Joan
have grown used to them.

Inside and out.

Diaphanous as scarves.
Drawn closer.

Sometimes, we even answer.
Glad we're not alone.

THE ORIGAMI OF TIME

for Martine Bellen

O how I love clocks,
                    their roundness.

Mother Time—

a drop of bright blood
enclosed in quartz
(cameo-like).

*

Behind their plain faces
one senses complexity.

Bewitching
in its folds
and creases.

Children play
near the edge.

Doves leap
from its high places.

JEROME MEDITATING

The eyes are closed.
The windows are open.
The blue towel is spread
in the center of the floor.

The windows are open.
The legs are crossed
in the center of the floor.
Shirtless. Shoeless.

The legs are crossed.
The chest is bare.
Shirtless. Shoeless,
with a hole in your left sock.

The chest is bare.
The skin pale.
With a hole in your left sock,
you count from one to ten.

The skin pale.
The breath steady.
You count from one to ten
like a child practicing scales.

The breath steady
in spite of thoughts that dart and swoop
like a child practicing scales
during rush hour.

In spite of thoughts that dart and swoop,
a single melody heard
during rush hour—
somewhere someone whistling an unfamiliar tune.

A single melody heard
comprised of all the noise, horns and birds.
Somewhere someone whistling an unfamiliar tune.
Then intermittent moments of calm.

Comprised of all the noise, horns, and birds,
discreetly a breeze enters the room.
Then intermittent moments of calm.
Hands resting on knees.

Discreetly a breeze enters the room
passing like a glance over
hands resting on knees,
books in piles all around.

Passing like a glance over—
what is it you are thinking now?
Books in piles all around:
Walter Benjamin and Meister Eckhart.

What is it you are thinking now,
at this moment, in this room—
Walter Benjamin? Meister Eckhart?
The incense continues to burn.

At this moment, in this room,
there's a vase of pussy willows behind your head.
The incense continues to burn,
but the candles remain unlit.

Yet even with pussy willows behind your head,
you seem sober, so absorbed.
The candles remain unlit
though the room grows dark.

You seen sober, so absorbed,
the stillness filling every corner
as the room grows dark
and I watch as if you were asleep.

The stillness filling every corner,
in the kitchen I put on water for tea
and watch as if you were asleep . . .
nothing but the sound of your heartbeat.

In the kitchen I put on water for tea,
aware of the echo each move makes.
Nothing but the sound of your heartbeat
like a shell bringing the ocean home.

from

THE CLOUD OF
KNOWABLE THINGS

NATIONAL POETRY MONTH

When a poem
speaks by itself,
it has a spark

and can be considered
part of a divine
conversation.

Sometimes the poem weaves
like a basket around
two loaves of yellow bread.

"Break off a piece
of this April with its
raisin nipples," it says.

"And chew them slowly
under your pillow.
You belong in bed with me."

On the other hand,
when a poem speaks
in the voice of a celebrity

it is called television
or a movie.
"There is nothing to see,"

says Robert De Niro,
though his poem bleeds
all along the edges

like a puddle
crudely outlined
with yellow tape

at the crime scene
of spring.
"It is an old poem," he adds.

"And besides,
 I was very young
 when I made it."

AUTOBIOGRAPHICAL POEM

The story of my skin
is long and involved.

While the story of my hair
is quite short.

In the story of my mouth
kisses linger over poppyseeds

and crumbs of lemon-scented cake.
There is a character who always builds

in the story of my bones
and a woman who refuses to leave

her gondola in the story of my blood.
But it is the heart's story

I most want to share
with you who also know this pleasure

of being shut inside
a vast dark place, alone—

as if at a small table
scribbling lies.

THE BANAL

Even with its shitload of artifacts, the everyday
is radiant, while the banal is opaque and often
obscure. I prefer the latter, with its murky
agate, mushroom, ochre background music—
its corridor of lurk. One hardly knows where
one stands with/in the banal. Walls come
together with hardly a seam. Wherever we are, we
feel we have always been. Poe, for all his special
effects, is rather banal in his approach to the
supernatural, i.e. overly familiar. Against the
inarticulate velvet of this mood, one grasps at
the everyday for relief. Thus any object can
bring us back with the fast-acting power of
aspirin. Any object shines.

THE SEVEN VEILS OF SPRING

1. ice water
2. egg yolk
3. pollen
4. cotton candy
5. fog
6. chablis
7. snot

Negative Capabilities

I'm not a landscape
but if I were I'd be a prairie
with wildflowers embroidered
on the yoke of my rippling.

I'm not a child
but if I were I'd want to be
a teaspoon, an eyedropper,
or a chandelier when I grow up.

I'm not a novel
but if I were I'd be by Kawabata
or Tanizaki. No one can match
the elegance of their melancholy.

ASKING FOR A RAISE

Perhaps there is a color
I can sleep in
like a spare room.

Some uncharted green.

Some state I'd gladly travel to
in the center of a loud noise
where all is calm.

Snug in my cupcake hut
the difference between
sleeping with pills

and sleeping without them
is the difference between
talking into a telephone
and talking into a jewel.

Depression is an economic state.
Green is also the color of cash.

"All right, but what would you do
with more money if you had it?"

asks the businessman who greets me
with a lei of orchids.

"Shop for clothes," I answer.
"And treat my husband like a whore."

I INTERVIEW ELAINE EQUI
ON THE FOUR ELEMENTS

Q: What is your favorite element?

A: Definitely air. It's the medium of thought.
   Ethereal. Invisible. And even better than air,
   I love heights. I'm the opposite of someone with
   acrophobia. Space travel sounds appealing.

Q: Which element do you like least?

A: Water. It makes me nervous. You can't walk on it.
   Both my parents are Pisces so perhaps that explains . . .
   I'm a terrible swimmer.

Q: Being a Leo, do you feel at home with fire?

A: I like light, but not heat. I don't even like hot
   sauce. I could never see myself as a pyromaniac.

Q: Which brings us to earth, what associations do you
   have with it?

A: The earth has always supported me in all my
   endeavors. I trust it.

Opaque Saints

We cannot see the fire within
that causes them to leap out of themselves
at inopportune moments

or stretch out on a bed of nails
with the blissful look of one
nursing on a lily.

So often, we too consider irrational acts
but wait holding our breath
until the moment passes.

Our boredom makes us happy then,
and Hell is the neat, well-organized place
from which we contemplate

the disruptive lives of saints
who break even natural laws.
Their faces are always luminous

and dry even when wet.
Their halos intrigue like jewelry
that can never be removed.

A QUIET POEM

My father screamed whenever the phone rang.

My aunt often screamed when she opened the door.

Out back, the willows caterwauled.

In the kitchen, the faucet screamed
a drop at a time.

At school, they called screaming "recess"
or sometimes "music."

Our neighbor's daughter had a scream
more melodious than my own.

At first, Col. Parker had to pay girls
to get them to scream for Elvis.

I didn't want to scream when I saw The Beatles,
but I did. After that, I screamed for even
mediocre bands.

Late in his career, John Lennon
got into Primal Scream.

Many people find it relaxing to scream.

Just as crawling precedes walking, so screaming
precedes speech.

The roller-coaster is just one of many
scream-inducing devices.

The ambulance tries, in its clumsy way, to emulate
the human scream, which in turn tries to emulate
nature.

Wind is often said to shriek, but Sylvia Plath
also speaks of "the parched scream of the sun."

Jim Morrison wanted to hear the scream of the
butterfly.

With ultra-sensitive equipment, scientists measure
the screams of plants they've tortured.

It's proven that if you scream at a person
for years, then suddenly stop, he will hear even
the tenderest words of love as violent curses.

And to anyone who speaks above a whisper, he will say:
"Don't you dare. Don't you dare raise your voice to me."

THE SENSUOUS READER

1.

In autumn
take all the red and blue
out of a book.

Make wine
for winter's
sharp profile.

Then trace the profile
of other objects
with a knife

the way wind does.

2.

Open any book
and look to see

if the author
is inside the words
your eyes caress.

Read backwards
and up and down.

Skim diagonally

or just glance at some parts
and not others.

3.

Read by

          flowerlight

          petal-flashlight

or make a big
Pentecostal bouquet
of fiery words.

4.

The Silent Partner:

For one whole day
carry a book everywhere—

but never open it.

5.

Buy some expensive chocolate.

Then go to the library
and whisper an author's name
(preferably dead) aloud.

Wait for them to arrive
or for something else to happen.

Variation on the above:
Eat the chocolate and go home.

THE OBJECTS IN CATALOGS

are made of light.
Well-lit or seemingly edible,
butterscotch and hazelnut light.
A bit vulgar, like starlets
the objects pose, pausing
as though in midsentence.
But really they are mute
—the story barely there.
Like children they wait to hear us
tell of the great Platonic love
we have for our many selves.
A vast literature reduced here
to a few short phrases: numbers,
letters, and of course, price.

The Objects in Japanese Novels

Empty cages outline
the periphery of an unnamed thing.
Their emptiness shines
like lanterns on virgin snow.
A few flakes swirl up,
caught—as scenic views
are caught in parts of speech,
where wishes and schemes
grow gloomy as a shrine,
and hair is a kind of incense.
Here, even abundance is delicate
with a slender waist.
And sorrow, embarrassment, disgust
can be aestheticized too
if surrounded by the right things—
a refreshing breeze, a small drum.

THE OBJECTS IN FAIRY TALES

are always
the most important
characters.
Then as now,
the power to transform
is theirs—
the story
a way of talking through
(and to) us.
Shoes of Fortune,
Magic Beans,
are unlike objects
in magazines
for they awaken
us against our will
from the spell of abject
longing for more.
Only then do we live
happily ever after.

2.

They speak
but not
to everyone,

just those
ready to hear
and endure

what they have to say—

impossible tasks,

shine wrapped around
the seedvoice.

Golden apples
in the grasp of time.

"I'll climb up."

3.

(we are)
          Forever turning

things into thoughts

or caught midair
dangling between

the way children
steep their toys
in imagination.

A bird's heart
in him.

Clouds will catch
and carry him off.

4.

But finally, the objects
in fairy tales are words.

Beautiful as any object
we re-call

"water"
                    "daughter"

Grazing down
in the cellar
through the window
to the face,

then the tall man
made a ring of himself,

flames
trembling like cold,

old skirt
              old stockings—

pride and arrogance.

"If you stretch yourself
you'll be there
in a couple of steps."

WITTGENSTEIN'S COLORS

Blond
Tamarind
Bacon
Fog

Burlap
Winter Grass
Semidark

Tarn
Goose
Nutmeg

Brown Light
Hot Blue

Lion's Mane
Liverspot
Birch

THE BURDEN OF BAD OBJECTS

"Bad floor," says the fallen child.

"Bad cloud," says the parade.

Bad dog. Bad penny.
Bad chemistry between the actors in a flop.

When he called me a moron, I was wearing my blue
sweater. Now *it* is bad.

Carnations always make me think of funerals.

The mirror upstairs adds ten years easy.

It's been a bad day.

Bad is a question of agency.
Bad is a matter of control.

We've all stood before rows of identical products
sensing one of them is bad.

Unless it is found and thrown away,
one bad object can ruin a whole life.

He erased his mistake and replaced it with the
correct answer.

She tore up every photograph where she didn't look
good.

MY TASTE

I hate being frugal.
I hate being extravagant.
Instead I prefer buying
small, useless things.
Like a hand reaching
into another century.
Carefully, I sharpen
the beaks of my pencil-birds
and fill in the sky.
Often, I feel I must
"buy back" everything
in order to recreate
some original state.
But other times, I shop
to make the world
an emptier place—
less embarrassed by its riches,
more aware of my grace.

EVERYWHERE TODAY WE SEE
A LACK OF COMMITMENT

Who was the original
actress—Joan Fontaine?
I got the feeling
she was a little more lost.
Like that scene where
she's looking down,
it seemed as if she
really might jump
or was thinking of jumping,
whereas this actress
just looked like:
"What do you mean JUMP?"

"YOUR PURPLE ARRIVES"

Purple flower.
               Purple heart.

Heap of sharp
and muddy edges.

Bruise or blossom?

Harp strings
trickle-down
realignment
of morning's slow . . .

bright bug
with a crumb of window
on its back.

O Patriarchy

Inaccessible
         and remote

behind the drawbridge
of the penis.

Who knows
how your contracts
sprang up

without a word,
natural as rain.

The institution
of you speaks
for all man kindly,

but if a woman
is offended,
she finds no one there
to blame.

THE KILLERS INSIDE ME

when they are off-duty
seem like anybody else
at a party or in a restaurant.

They could even be witty
or give good advice
on which shoes to buy,

i.e. open-toe gladiator sandals
work best for celestial power-walking.

Really, they are not bad
when not cruelly maiming.

From now on, I've adopted
a live-and-let-live policy
toward the killers inside me.

WOMEN AND MAGIC

A woman
in a wavy room
changes into starlight

as silence lifts
its hat
        in passing

and this
we call occult.

EARLY INFLUENCE

My mother lives *between* other people's words.

On TV they say this.
In the newspaper that.

Even those closest to her, when they speak,
are like a landscape she moves through
half-listening, unimpressed.

Not that she's unfeeling or aloof,
only that she prefers colors, flavors, textures—
prefers to draw or paint, cook, sew.

She doesn't know how easily,
just by picking up a pen,
their words become *yours*.

She isn't interested in such a transfer.

I've always admired this imperiousness,
this resistance to the so-called power of words.

It is perhaps her most political act
and one I find useful to recall when writing.

FURNITURE FANTASY

Homeless club kids
living on rice, beans,
and Gitanes.

All day he forces them
to strip
          paint,

sand hutches,
and stain armoires
to the music of Billie Holiday.

Outdoors, under a tarp,
even in rain.
All this they gladly do
without complaint

for how else
will the owner
know whose love
of antiques is true

and who's a fake—

which urchin
to take
to his ancient
mahogany sleigh bed

and which to make
curl up in
the Morris chair.

Take-Out Fantasy

He left a rodeo
to answer the phone.

Merely an expediter:
laconic tumbleweed
in the kitchen of desire.

He rolls the same phrases
over and over.

"Where to?"
"What'll you have?"
"You got it."

So picture him
in a leather jacket
over sweat-soaked skin,

his fly open—
his voice rubbing in
the extra hot sauce.

"Two onion rings, one
guacamole, one diet coke.
What else?"

Never angry or judgmental.
Never elsewhere.

To the almost unbearable
question of "what do you want?"

he brings utter simplicity—
                    efficiency.

Calm as someone
high in the mountains,
he speaks reassuringly:

"Fifteen minutes."
"You got it."
"Buh-bye."

ALIEN FANTASY

I wouldn't mind being naked
in their pupil-less eyes.

Just think of them coming all that way
for nothing but a closer look

as if Earth were one big peep show
advertising LIVE FLESH, LIVE FLESH

in undulating neon telepathy.
Who could be as fascinated

by our sloppy existence?
Who could care less about what is art

as they mix semen and stardust
or goose our boredom with joyride's probe.

And busy as we are, how else to justify
leaving work except in a crazy abduction

scenario? You check your schedule
again and again. Lost forever—

those four hours—like ancient teenagers
wander in some glittering arcade.

OUT OF THE CLOUD CHAMBER

and into the street.

Out of the art-deco prison
and into the cozy burning house,
the bleak house,
           the decadent steak house.

Out of the mouths of tulips and slaves.

Out of the frying pan and into the choir.

Out of mimesis endlessly mocking.

Out like a debutante,
          in like a thief.

Out of pocket,
          out of reach.

Out of time
          and into being.

Out of sight
          and into seeing.

Out of your mind
          and into your pants.

Out like a light
          and in like a lamp.

The Lost Poems

Your Average Dream
Fetish-Shroud
Victor Mature's Kiss
The Snow Queen's Summer House

In a Nutshell
De-composing
Vintage Blouse
Politics and Vaseline

Mister Preface
Charm-Quake
Postponing the Future
Notice Each Part

The Cloud's Tantrum
Harlequin With a Gun

A Bend in the Light

A bend in the light.
A dross in the drift.
A tilt in the storm.
A gleam in the ditch.

A grace in the gloom.
A kink in the sand.
A spring in the fire.
A lilt in the hand.

A snare in the common.
A hare in the shed.
A mesh in the fury.
A glare in the blurring.

A stretch in the arc.
A pulse in the bark.
A fork in the wave.
A heft in the sway.

INTERSECTIONS

I'm at the corner of Can't & Won't.
In the kiosk between Aroma & Automatic,

Squirm & Squall,
Minimal Art & Minimum Wage.

I'm trying to get to Hilt & Vine.
The high-priestess in the high-rise

and the persona in the persona-non-grata dept.
both told me that if I cut across Performance

& Fugue, Mayday & Kind, it would put me
on the quad next to the grid

near Bittersweet & Icarus
and from there I could walk.

A Sentimental Song

We feel more than see
the stars white as radishes
and as sharp.

To we who always look down,
it's right that they be *in* the ground.
We love winter because it makes inner

seem even more inner
                              and crackling.

*

Cold is a fragrance
that clings to the skin
and smells cold.

Imagine a perfume called "Snow"
and another called "Drizzle"
and another called "January"

and all of them—free.

*

Just for today, I'd like to
step into someone else's list.
Run their errands. Wish their wish.

Today is St. Ita's day (the most famous
woman saint in Ireland after Brigid).
She is said to have reattached

the head to the body
of a man who'd been beheaded
and to live only on food from heaven.

Meanwhile the weather here is gray
but optimistic, aspiring to (I'm not sure what).
The slant of something moving up and away.

TRENTON LOCAL

for Susan Wheeler

Crows ride slow
rafts of ice downstream:
Barge music

under sky's
low ceiling

Openings
open one after
another

Wreaths of space
crown weeds, thorns

You start in
the middle. You start
again here.

Factory
                    Reverie

Shadowplay
behind the scrim of
production

Crime, sex, art
greed, and sports

One story
gets folded into
another

Even trees
play a part

Enhancing
the lullaby of
certain words

repeated
        precisely

O wall that
asks eternally
"SKEETER, WHY?"

I love your
lurid scrawl!

Yellow meets
and mingles with me
and dark red

Courthouse flag
waves good-bye

Cables sag
and stretch to meet their
connections

Spring is a
station too

She scribbles
on watery screens,
sheets of air . . .

feather-pen
        quarter notes

The jagged
lace of broken glass
unweaving

Billboards talk
vis-à-vis

So where is
this invisible
leading man?

scattered in
        time and place

Four brides left
forever in the
bridal shop

Ashes cloud milk.
Mist veils rocks.

Train's motion
makes the landscape seem
to tremble

A girl in
blue, smoking

Wedged in—this
time you start closer
to the end

Not wanting
to arrive

The hills of
empty packaging
dazzle us

A shrine to
appetite

We've consumed
all that and still are
ravenous.

Feeding our
frustration

"The best part
of my day would be
the bagel."

Sloppy and
        Mythical

A soft vague
border between speech
and silence

between the
wild and tame

To dream of
a tunnel suggests
birth or death

Gravediggers
work in shades.

Is it jade
or black—the river's
lost mood ring?

Paper fish
scale the sky

Spare car parts
spread out like bones to
be sun-dried

Gears caught in
the crabgrass

What is elf
lubricant? And where
can I buy?

Winter's quick
cameo

A whistle
that never sounds the
same way twice

DESSERT

This caramel is scriptural.
This lemon tart more beautiful than a Matisse.
It's the way paintings (and heaven) taste
as they dissolve and we internalize them.

Gurus know it.
Don't you remember after they slapped us
with peacock-feather-fans,
the little piece of rock candy
we each got and sucked in the corner,
thinking that if the mantras didn't work,
at least there was this.

For August in April

Now that we are back
to the beginning
of the alphabet—

its green apron
                and aquarium days,

its archers who aim
                at nothing at all,

who prefer to let
the targets come to them.

Suddenly, we are ashamed
of trying to connect things
with artifice and would prefer
the actor speak his part
in a series of asides.

We aspire to an assortment.

The asylum shines
                with symptoms

that are, at first, at attention
then later, at ease

as if consciousness
were nothing but an auction house.

The radio is not on, yet
much is still audible—

                auguries, aubades.

RETURN OF THE SENSUOUS READER

Reading Nude vs. Reading Barefoot

Unless you are especially comfortable
with your body, reading in the nude is likely
to be more of a distraction than an enhancement.

A better compromise that still lends an air of ease
and intimacy is reading barefoot. Just imagine
walking barefoot over the words you're reading.
Note: this is especially pleasurable to do in public.

Turning Down the Sound

Remove all the words from a poem;
keep only the punctuation.

Can You Recognize This Famous Poem?

,

.

.

A sublime treat for purists
or good exercise to cleanse the palate.

The Text as Symptom

Read the same poem at different times
and record your response in terms of
purely physical sensations: heartbeat, pulse, etc.

Warning: hypochondriacs, don't get carried away
with this one.

Does It Make Any Difference?

Change the gender of all the pronouns in a poem
and see for yourself.

Against Memorization

Memorizing a poem is a good way to destroy it.
You think it will bring you closer (like getting
a tattoo) but the poem does not reside in its words
and that is all you'll be left with.

Never again will you encounter it by chance
in the casual cruising-space that spells romance.
Rereading works better.

All Books Are Oracles

Formulate your question.
Use the standard open-at-random-
and-point method.

Live according to the words.

AFTER AND IN KEEPING WITH H.D.

When I am a current
               lifted up—
can you hear eclipses' seasoning?

When you are a cure-all,
there is no signal,
                   nor sorcery
trailing along.

When I am a curve-ball
                 made of shelter,
O can you hear distance receding?

When you are a comment,
there is no sour cherry
trudging across sanctuary gravel.

CAREER

In trees

the leaves have
finally found
their niche.

RESET

Fingers
    and page

stained saffron
with first light.

Flight the swoop
of cars below, the war whoop
of birds casting spells.

The man of pipes
and the man of ladders
ascend, descend, then find a level.

Putting one's head in the clouds,
one realizes how stubborn they (clouds) are—
how long they take to move,

the way they insist,
with their many-colored inks,
on writing backwards

    *

Balcony

Three empty
beer bottles rest
side by side
in the nest
of a cinderblock
of tall wild grass.

Beside a ragged palm
a ratty rattan chair
leans forward.

Like an old couple
the white plastic chairs
are pushed close.
Their arms touch gently.

*

Humming a nondescript incandescence,
the city runs itself without need of words.
I dreamt last night of a choice between two things

(A & B) but can't remember what they were
or which I decided on. One had certain features,
the other was just darkness.

Mornings are so dazzling, I hadn't noticed
this quality in them before and only wanted
to prolong night for as long as possible, forever.

It seems I've never carried anything this heavy
up a flight of stairs: worlds piggybacked
upon worlds. Every ocean a drop in the bucket.

But you didn't try to persuade me to put it down.
You said: "Look, what you carry is an image.
How much can an image possibly weigh?"

*

Periodically,
Miro-like
blue stick-figures

walk across
the sky

like matches
waiting to be lit.

Connect
the turquoise dots.

Ash & Rain.

Decorators do different things
with rooftops.

One makes a Roman arch
complete with tendrils of grapes.

Another is simply
a stage set

for automatons'
pas de deux.

A little of this.
A little of postmodernist that.

*

Dreamt I visited Mi Casa Roja.
Mi Casita Rojita.
My little pink cottage—

a Mexican restaurant
where they show videos
of my old poetry readings

but I can't get a table.
The waiters, the customers
everyone in my own cunt too busy to see me!

Finally, found a woman I knew and read
a passage aloud to her about candlelight.
"You know how I feel about candlelight."

Later, walked with swaying hips up stairs
followed by an anonymous, clove-scented man.
As in most movies, I never got to see what we did.

Mi Casa Roja: perhaps I will visit you again soon.

*

    Last night, it wasn't dreams I remembered but
falling asleep and this morning—waking. The back
and forth of it, prolonging those two states so as
to be able to re-create them again.
    We are at war. How old-fashioned it sounds, bor-
rowed from another century. Yet today, even the
weather is bureaucratically gray. The buildings so
suddenly officious under all their flags. One hangs
listless from a window, more like laundry meant to
dry than majestic. Another tiny flag waves atop the
watertower's drab cabana.

In the background is the sound of hammering
and all around, the feel of those larger-than-life
striding above the city, busy. Then, just before I
came in, a small mustache of light appeared like
the aphorism of a quick kiss.

*

Tarpaper
beaded
with water.

A centipede
crosses a line.
The sun
crosses a line too.

Went higher up this morning
onto a ledge I hadn't noticed
and found the Yellow Pages
open to "T"

Taj Mahal
Talent Partners
Talk To The Hand Inc.
Tangerine Café
Target Trading
Tattoo Photography
Tell It To A Star

Wonder who they were trying to call?
Wonder who *they* is?

Chilly wind keeps slamming the door open
like a ghost. Keeps turning the pages

of my notebook. Rereading: "Mornings
are so dazzling. I hadn't noticed this
quality in them before." Yet now know
every pebble, powder-puff-plant, paint smudge

as if by name, whispered. One always aesthetically
pleasing moment is when a dove settles on the
forest-green trim of the Win Restaurant Supply Co.
across the street. Or when sun lights the bricks
of an adjacent building turning them a deep salmon.

*

Cold Lookout

Sky
        a graveyard.

Ours is a city
of writing implements.

For nearly fifty years
I've been at war
with my body—

its explosive
women's ways.

When young
I always wanted to be
first a martyr—
then a spy.

One who moved
through fall colors

with a secret plan,

blank sheet of paper
carefully folded
in my pocket.

I like blending in
but should there be
someone watching
all they'd see is a hooded figure
on a rooftop.

Mala beads in gloved hands.
Lips moving.

I plant my syllables in light.
Let them multiply there.

How purposefully
everyone walks
the shadow-splashed streets
as if on their way
to a new job.

No loitering.

10/18/01 – 11/9/01

Variations on the Horizon

In the morning he was Apollo or Ra—

the ancient one, but by noon he was just plain
Yahweh, and by evening, Sly, a nameless gust
who played the wind chimes increasing the
number of ants on the march, vociferous as all
get-out beneath their shag carpet of flame.
Miles turned the rotisserie until the book was
charred and black. Knowledge back then was
edible and served on the backs of broad green
leaves. The Kabbalists kept count of everything.
That were their way. Some wrote buildings and
tried to rewrite the stairway but the banister
broke off in my hand—soggy and splintered and
solipsistic. Still, I liked the way it continued like
a church picnic with no church to return to.
Perhaps I was flattered to think my presence
made some sort of contribution or that I was
touched by something improvisational yet all
worked out. Almost but not quite . . . almost
but not quite

                    the ever-elusive,
                       Mr. & Mrs. Spirit

EARLY WORK

from

VIEWS WITHOUT ROOMS
ACCESSORIES
THE CORNERS OF THE MOUTH
SHREWCRAZY
FEDERAL WOMAN

OKAY

Often she built
a whole stage

just to say
      "okay"

Props
      waterfalls

cue cards

they would
tell her

quit making
a production
out of everything

then she would
say it
      "okay"

The Monster Dances

tossing its
three
pretty heads

in three directions
at once

then lowering
them in unison

as with
the grand and
measured walk
of a Borgia
it goes about
destroying
the city

CANNIBALS IN SPACE

Although they fashioned
their spears
on the lathe
of our technology

we had to admit
we liked watching them

with their bare chests
and heavy metal candor
they lent a sort of
backyard charm
to the universe

until even the doctor
and his assistant

were snapping their fingers
nodding their heads and
using everything they knew
about reality
to help them escape

POEM BEGINNING WITH A
LINE BY JAMES WRIGHT

"Relieved, I let the book fall behind a stone."
My friends are all at work.
My relatives, out of town.
Alone, I spend the afternoon reading
books of bad poetry and bad stories.
It is more soothing than listening
to the banter of cockroaches
as they drag off with heavy legs
the light and shadowy crumbs of my pancake.
For even in bad books, there are good words,
malice and throbbing. Relieved,
I let the book fall behind a stone
where it grows altogether shady and inviting.
On afternoons such as this
I do not want Rilke's angels in my mirror
or Kafka showing his narrow chest.
On afternoons such as this
I want to share my bed with bad books,
warm and unpredictable adolescents.

THE MOST BEAUTIFUL BLONDE IN THE WORLD

All day long she's been appearing.
Visions of Marilyn Monroe
during brunch, at tea,
and for my midnight snack.

Waiters hand me her autograph.
Clerks throw in the nude calendar spread
along with my buttons.
Is it possible that she is seeking me out?
And just when I was beginning to lose interest.

Marilyn in blue bathing suit
tugging a rope that rings a little bell
somewhere in heaven where I am
walking on clouds.

Her initials are M & M,
melts in your mouth
and mine are E E,
easily entertained.
Together that spells me.

Me, as in, "If you still want me, I'm all yours!"
Yes, she really said that.
And I told her, I'd think it over.

ODE TO CHICAGO

In my city
dinosaurs are not extinct.
Evenings they stroll downtown
and their smooth bodies
from the fortieth floor
are often mistaken for golf courses.
Pterodactyls swoop
above our vegetarian restaurants
while in the park
the famous sea serpent
entices tourists with his lewd chatter,
his long neck.
Nowhere else will you find rocks that perspire,
trees that grow hair.
Here even the common criminal
loves to talk about his "primeval mother"
and although some refer to it as uncivilized,
in my city we know where we come from.
We remember our origins.

CLOWN

It was an exciting thing
for a guy like him to become a clown overnight.
For a while, he was quite a success.
You wouldn't believe how many people saw him.
Only he didn't know any games
or funny things to say.
He would just show up at kids' parties
looking weird
and sit there.

THEN I BECAME
THE WEATHERGIRL

The air is full of secrets.
Just by breathing,
you become my accomplice.

For Hollis Sigler

"I got this job
 being a woman"
 but I could
 just as easily
 have been a hammock
 practicing swaying and shade.
 I could have been
 coral or old wine.
 Meanwhile, in the city
 men are dancing with tape measures.
 Building things
 without any flowers.
 When they're done,
 they'll want to hire some women.

Waiting on You

after Neruda

I'm tired of the red restaurant
and the blue restaurant.
Tired of the green one under the sign of the parrot.
I'm tired of the restaurant in the sky
whose name is spelled wrong for eternity.
I've worked at them all,
carried your dinners there through the woods,
swept away bones. As it happens,
I'm tired of being a waitress.

Tired of the dirty dishes
which gather themselves together
like a congregation waiting to be cleansed.
Tired of the greasy horizon
and the sun's pompous belly.
Tired of the foreign accents like the buzz
of Italian, Greek, and Chinese flies,
of the stink of forty separate countries
dying in a single ashtray.

As it happens, I'm tired of being a waitress,
of parading myself before men, women,
whole families raised on garbage and tacky décor.
Tired of the wishing well, the clean cup.
Tired of men's rooms, ladies' rooms, candlelight, ketchup.

Tired of snobs and shy ones.
I no longer want to be
the person who has good manners in hell.

Friends, it's not your appetites
that disgust me. I, too, wish
that a woman was a glass of champagne
but we're fooling ourselves.

Why not go back to being cannibals?
Why not drink nothing but our mother's milk?

Yes or No

One day I looked up
and the answer was there
in the sky,
it was no.
You were like a No
dancing above the city
to Chopin,
gray as a plume of smoke.
Like a plant in the winter light
you leaned the wrong way
with eyes radiant
as a ladybug's.
And we all knew together
at that moment,
the woman carrying her bag of oranges
across the street
and the man photographing the sun,
we knew whatever the question might be,
its answer was definitely—no.

HI-FASHION GIRL

I'm swinging through a department store of the future
because by then it will be possible to do that. I mean hear
red. Dig the brass section of this cra-zy shirt.
Wait a minute, if this is the future, why am I talking
like a ridiculous beatnik poet? The past must be following
too close behind. Lodged by the cosmetics like a little
Vietnamese girl with a grenade under her dress.
I'd offer chocolate but in the department store of the
future all they sell is the potential for candy.
The potential to make mom happy on her birthday.
The potential to look terrific. What is all this potential
I keep seeing like landscape in a recurring weirdo dream?
It must be the reason I ask you to style my hair, order my meals,
and supervise the movies I see. Yes, so I'll be ready
for the next big trend after death. Glass elevators where you
do ascend into heaven but are only kept around to serve champagne.
Man, that is not modern. That was done in the dark ages.

ARRANGED AFFAIR

What type of body would you have if you could
gain time instead of weight? I mean
rather than counting calories, you'd count .001's
of a second. The 19th century being equal to a banana split,
the 20th a Big Mac. It's known that Einstein would eat
his way into the future, copy down the equations he was
famous for, then diet frantically trying to throw up
the excess years. But he stopped too soon.
By going even further, one can see The Great Famine
where everything gets reduced to zero. By that time
all the animals have grown thin as illustrations.
Then numbers will be remembered as the last great religion.
A giant 1+1 smoldering with incense. Black, as if branded
on a birthday cake. A place so private no one will find us.

AMBER STREET

If I want you to listen to me and you don't want to,
is it okay to break both your legs until I'm finished talking?
I know some people don't approve of this method,
but where do you end up leaving things to chance?
A loser, mumbling the Kama Sutra. On the other hand,
applause from a wheelchair may sound a little hollow,
but I'd still rather take home a dying rose
than a guy who can't talk about anything besides his ex-wife.
By now, it should be obvious, I'll get the chamber pot of gold,
and even if it turns to shit, never give it back.
Forgive me, I'm not trying to show different ways to lose.
I just want a room full of grizzly trophies,
a closet full of shrunken heads that sing.
Then when company comes, instead of criticizing my bad taste,
they'll say, "Poor thing, that's all she lives for."
And after that all I'll need to complete the scenario
is a boiled shrimp in ruffles so I can say,
"If it wasn't for my kid, I wouldn't be worth a damn."

POEM

We got all kinds of things
in the Windy City. Mostly
terrible.

       Me no wheeler dealer.

       Me no mailman.

       Me go racing with the gods in purple
Cadillacs. Pass by beauty parlor, my hair
just the right shade of yellow. I knew
if I didn't make it, my shoes would.

DOLOR

Dolor—sadness kept as a powder in small jars
sometimes distinguished by a Greek label
and scented with vanilla.
As in the sentence:
he drave her away and took out his jar of dolor.

Friable—easily crumbled:
the dolor was friable to a point.

Depute—appoint to do one's work:
when the dolor was missing, strangers were deputed
to recover it.

A PLAN

Call the weatherlady often. In fact,
think of every phone booth as your private property.
Sell surgical supplies or lingerie during the day
but at night invent weapons from the pieces of broken
toasters. Listen to the national anthem but
avoid experts and the police.
Have photographs taken at places you ordinarily wouldn't,
in a sailboat if you dislike water etc.
To protect against rust, line the inside of your coat
with tinfoil. Alternate between using the first and
third person when dining alone in a restaurant.
Say, "I'll have a cheeseburger; give her a Coke."
Learn to forge the signatures of dead celebrities.
Tell your friends you'll just be gone for the weekend.
Remember I have confidence in you.
This time you'll do it.

Notes & Acknowledgments

NEW WORK

Some of these poems first appeared in *American Poetry Review, The Brooklyn Rail, Coconut, Conjunctions, Court Green, Gulf Coast, The New Yorker, Poem Memoir Story, The Tiny, TriQuarterly,* and *Vanitas.* "Pre-Raphaelite Pinups" was included in *The Best American Poetry 2005,* edited by Paul Muldoon and David Lehman.

from SURFACE TENSION

"A Date with Robbe-Grillet" was included in *The Best American Poetry 1989,* edited by Donald Hall and David Lehman.

from DECOY

"Dear Michael" is addressed to poet Michael Lally. "Sometimes I Get Distracted" was included in *The Best American Poetry 1995,* edited by Richard Howard and David Lehman.

from VOICE-OVER

"Wang Wei's Moon" is a cento composed entirely of lines about moonlight by the T'ang dynasty poet, Wang Wei. All are from wonderful translations done by Tony Barnstone, Willis Barnstone, and Xu Haixin. "From Lorine" is a collage of lines and phrases (slightly edited) from Lorine Niedecker's letters. "Voice-Over" contains quotes from The Psychic Readers Network, The Faith and Values Network, an ad for Royal Caribbean Cruise Ships, and Andre Breton's *Manifestoes of Surrealism.*

from THE CLOUD OF KNOWABLE THINGS

"Your Purple Arrives" is a line taken from Louis Zukofsky. "The Sensuous Reader" and "Return of the Sensuous Reader" were inspired by the sexy, self-help classic *The Sensuous Woman* and its sequel—both by "J". The August of "For August in April" refers not only to the eighth month of the year, but also to one of my favorite poets, August Kleinzahler. "After and In Keeping With H.D." is a rewrite of an H.D. poem called "When I Am a Cup." "Reset" was written as a response to a prescription for insomnia given me by a doctor who suggested that I sit in the sun, facing east, for one hour each morning in order to reset my inner clock. I chose the roof of my apartment building as the site for this ritual. "O Patriarchy" was included in *The Best American Poetry 2002*, edited by Robert Creeley and David Lehman.

from EARLY WORK

"For Hollis Sigler" begins with the line "I got this job being a woman," which is the title of a painting by this extraordinary Chicago artist.

COLOPHON

Ripple Effect was designed
at Coffee House Press,
in the historic warehouse district
of downtown Minneapolis.
Fonts include Bodoni and Iowan Old Style.

FUNDER ACKNOWLEDGMENT

Coffee House Press is an independent nonprofit literary publisher. Our books are made possible through the generous support of grants and gifts from many foundations, corporate giving programs, individuals, and through state and federal support. This book has received special project support from the National Endowment for the Arts, a federal agency. Coffee House Press receives general operating support from the Minnesota State Arts Board, through an appropriation by the Minnesota State Legislature and from the National Endowment for the Arts, and major general operating support from the McKnight Foundation, and from the Target Foundation. Coffee House also receives support from: an anonymous donor; the Elmer and Eleanor Andersen Foundation; the Buuck Family Foundation; the Patrick and Aimee Butler Family Foundation; Gary Fink; Stephen and Isabel Keating; the Lenfesty Family Foundation; Rebecca Rand; the law firm of Schwegman, Lundberg, Woessner & Kluth, P.A.; the James R. Thorpe Foundation; the Archie D. and Bertha H. Walker Foundation; Thompson West; the Woessner Freeman Family Foundation; Wood-Rill Foundation; and many other generous individual donors.

This activity is made possible in part by a grant from the Minnesota State Arts Board, through an appropriation by the Minnesota State Legislature and a grant from the National Endowment for the Arts. MINNESOTA STATE ARTS BOARD

NATIONAL ENDOWMENT FOR THE ARTS

To you and our many readers across the country, we send our thanks for your continuing support.

Good books are brewing at coffeehousepress.org

ABOUT THE AUTHOR

Born in Oak Park, Illinois, Elaine Equi grew up in Chicago and the outlying suburbs and graduated from Columbia College. Before moving to New York in the 1980s, she and her husband, poet Jerome Sala, did numerous readings together, helping to create Chicago's lively performance poetry scene. Over the years, her witty, aphoristic, and innovative work has become nationally and internationally known.

Equi is the author of more than ten poetry collections, including *Voice-Over*, which won a San Francisco State University Poetry Center Award. Widely published and anthologized, her work has appeared in *The New Yorker, American Poetry Review, Postmodern American Poetry: A Norton Anthology,* and numerous volumes of *The Best American Poetry.* She lives in New York City where she teaches at New York University and in the MFA programs at The New School and City College.